To Eleanor
with a lot
of love !

xxx Evi Gia

15/10/20

C000039607

EVI GIAKOUMI

ABOUT LOVE AND LIFE
POEMS

AKAKIA 2012

AKAKIA Publications
St Peters Vicarage
Wightman Road
London N8 0LY, UK
0044 203 28 66 550
0044 7411 40 65 62
www.akakia.net
publications@akakia.net

Evangelia Giakoumi
ABOUT LOVE AND LIFE
Poems

Cover Image:
Photo taken by Evangelia Giakoumi 2012

ISBN: 978-1-909550-28-5

London, UK

CONTENTS

This anthology has in it hidden bits of my heart. Produced with a lot of love at a time in my life where the birth of my son Lucas filled me with pride, joy, love and gratitude. So to him it is dedicated with all my heart. And to his father Filipe, who gave me such a wonderful boy.

I love you both!

The Highest Top

I went up one day
on the highest top.
My life from there
I liked a lot.

Whatever I feared,
neared and loathed
showed me to love
the winding road.

My troubles up there
seemed rather small,
no worry or fear
to spoil my ball.

I then went back down
whistling and humming,
all happy and ready
to start again living.

Another Year

Another year
to bring together
the joys and sorrows
for all to remember.

We've done a lot,
but there's still more to come.
All the excitement
and fun we'll have.

Every year
hides precious treasures,
no need to fear
stresses and pressures.

With Love and Patience
everything is easy,
problems and hurdles
give Life a meaning.

Noone Knows

Who really knows
what life will bring?
The thrill of the unknown
brightens everything.

From the beginning
until the end,
follow the journey
and don't regret.

Life will surprise you
when no one expects,
will break and wake you.
The story never ends.

A Whole Life

Life isn't fair,
but is also unpredictable.
You win and then you lose
and that isn't despicable.

Naked and alone
you see a baby born,
how life may treat her
is not foreseen at all.

The joys and the memories
that everybody holds
are theirs, no-one can claim them.
They're theirs and theirs alone.

Keep Going

I fall and rise
I cry and smile
I shout and whisper
I run and try.

I pray and talk
I feel and hold
I cry and smile
I fall and rise.

New Beginnings

There is no beginning
without an end,
there is no mistake
in an amend.

Life's true meaning
is a deep puddle,
the real happiness
comes through the rubble.

Without pain
there is no gain,
to find something
try lose everything.

Answers

Don't look for answers
in every problem,
when in your mind
there is no point.

Sometimes things
are meant to be,
look deep inside you
and set them free.

Although we want to
and really wish,
we cannot change
what we'd rather miss.

Face every challenge
with a fresh glance.
Don't let your life
go into chance.

And Then What?

What happens when the lights are gone,
what if you feel you've done it all?
Who really cares what was your fault,
where does your duty stop?

What if you think your love is lost,
your roots forgotten, your future told?
What happens when the wheel is spun,
you got a zero and lost the fun?

What do you do without hope,
who do you turn to and get a rope?
To carry you up out of the hole,
mend you and make you again whole?

No Tomorrow

If I didn't have tomorrow,
what is that I would miss the most?

Which hands would I like to have
inside of mine closed?

Which face, what place,
what song to sing?

What book to read,
which film to see?

Whose eyes to meet,
which heart to reach?

Where would I go, what would I do,
who would I be with?

Conquering

Think with your head,
love with your heart,
live with your soul,
stay forever young.

When you're feeling down,
don't forget to smile.
When you're feeling proud,
put your hopes aside.

Aim in conquering
what you always wanted.
Don't allow fail
make you feel forgotten.

Princess

He calls me his Princess.
He says I'm the one.
I asked for forgiveness
and got none but one.

Did none to deserve this.
I sin and demand.
Had begged for redemption,
I found what I asked.

Angel

Be strong and be brave,
let the candle burn forever
and warm your broken hearts.
May the time go by fast.

Bring your angel back to you,
soothe her and relieve you too,
take you out of the dark.
Pray to God to bring her back.

To Hold You

I learn and you learn,
we both grow together.
My hand in your hand,
could it stay forever?

I blocked the world
to have you and hold you.
I ask for no more
than nurture and love you.

In another life
I would again find you.
My hand in your hand,
could I stay beside you?

About the Author

Evi Giakoumi was born in Komotini, Greece in 1974. She grew up in Athens and Mytilene, where she lived until 1999. She then decided to move to the UK, where she did her postgraduate studies in Environmental Engineering. After working in engineering for ten years and following the birth of her son Lucas, she turned to education and writing. The writer created her first poetry book "About love and life" between 2009 and 2012.

The writer's first Greek poetry collection named "Tarakse ta nera" (Make a splash) is also published by AKAKIA Publications.

Made in the USA
Charleston, SC
30 January 2013